# Making Music

Heather Hammonds

## Contents

# Music for Everyone

Music is found all over the world.

We can listen to music.
We can play music, too.

Music can be played
by one person
or by lots of people.

Music can be played on **musical instruments**.

*These musical notes
show different
musical sounds.*

# Music from Strings

Some musical instruments have strings. Musical sounds are made when the strings move quickly back and forth.

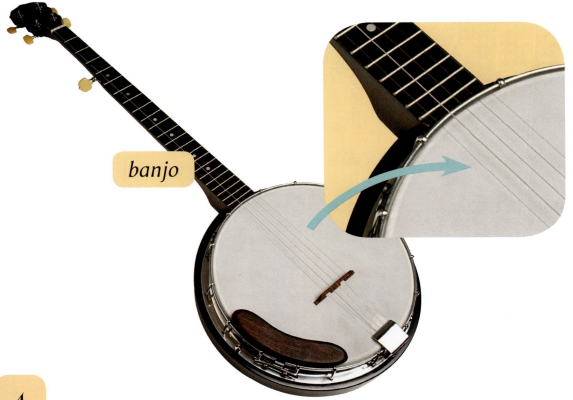

banjo

This boy is playing the guitar.
His music teacher is showing him what to do.

This guitar has six strings.

This musical instrument has strings, too.
It is much smaller than a guitar.

violin

All these musical instruments have strings.

double bass

cello

viola

Did you know that a piano has strings inside it?

Chapter 3

# Music from Air

Some musical instruments are played by blowing air into them.

*panpipes*

This boy is playing the recorder.
He makes high or low sounds
by blowing into the recorder
and covering the holes with his fingers.

*These recorders were
made long ago.*

This musical instrument is played by blowing into it.

The **musician** holds it to the side when he is playing it.

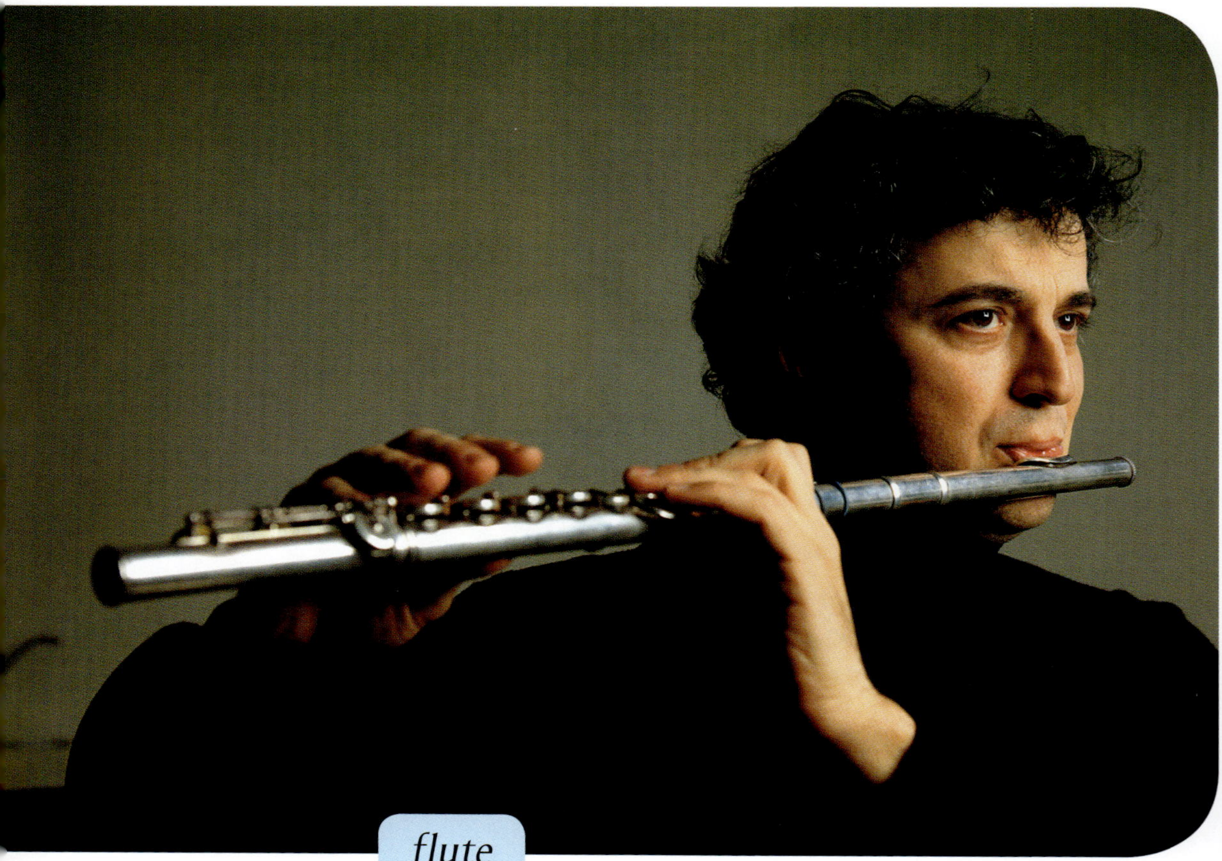

*flute*

All these musical instruments are played by blowing into them.

saxophone

bassoon

Some are big, and some are small.

clarinet

piccolo

These musical instruments are called **woodwind** instruments.

flute

11

# Chapter 4

# Big Brass Sounds

Look at the musical instruments in this marching band.

The marching band plays music as it marches along.

This boy is playing the trumpet.
The trumpet is a loud instrument.

These musical instruments
are called **brass**
instruments.

tuba

Part of this musical instrument slides in and out when it is played.

trombone

This brass instrument is very big and heavy.
Sometimes the musician sits down to play it.

tuba

Here are some more
brass instruments.

French horn

flugelhorn

Brass instruments are played by blowing air
into them.

# Chapter 5

# Taps and Beats

Some musical instruments are played with **mallets**,

glockenspiel

bongos

or with your hands,

cymbals

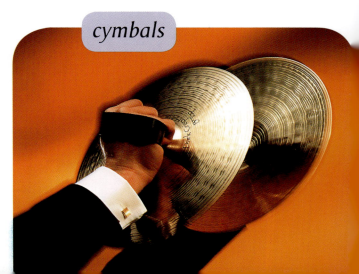

or by hitting them together.

This girl is playing the drums.
She plays the drums with drumsticks.

*You can also play the drums with these special brushes.*

This musical instrument
is played with mallets.
The musician hits the bars
with the mallets.

These musical instruments make lots of sounds. Have you ever played any of them?

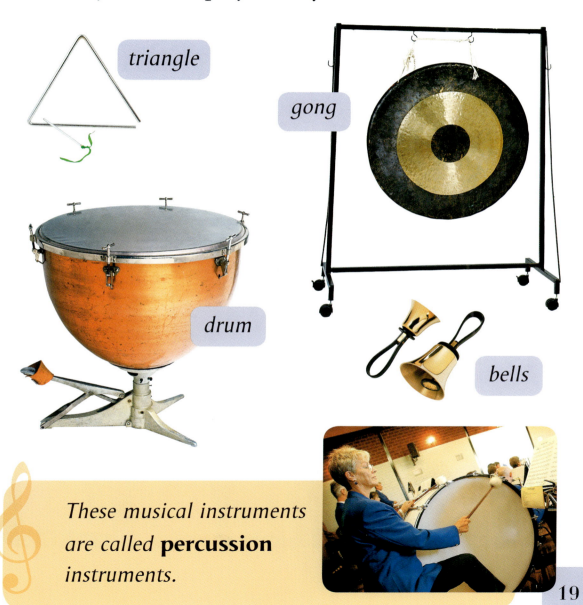

triangle

gong

drum

bells

These musical instruments are called **percussion** instruments.

# Chapter 6

# Playing Together

When lots of musical instruments
are played together, they sound very good!

These children play in a band.
They like to play music together.

Lots of people are playing musical instruments in this **orchestra**.

Everyone has a special place in the orchestra.

*The **conductor** helps the orchestra to play together.*

# Chapter 7

# A World of Music

Music is played all over the world with lots of musical instruments.

*mandolin*

*bagpipes*

*digeridoo*

We can buy musical instruments.
We can make musical instruments.

We can make music by singing, too!
Singing together is fun.

# Glossary

| | |
|---|---|
| **brass** | a kind of metal |
| **conductor** | a person who tells the musicians in an orchestra or band what to do |
| **mallets** | sticks with round heads used for playing certain musical instruments |
| **musical instruments** | special tools that play music |
| **musician** | a person who plays music |
| **orchestra** | a group of musicians who play string, brass, woodwind, and percussion instruments together |
| **percussion** | a kind of instrument that makes a sound when a part of it is struck |
| **woodwind** | a kind of instrument that may be made of wood and is played by blowing air into it |

# Index